India For Kids: Amazing Facts About India
By Shalu Sharma

Table of Contents

What is India?

India is a big country in South Asia. This country is a republic and its history goes back many centuries. On 15 August 1947, India became independent from British rule. India celebrates its Republic Day every year on 26th January, the day it got its constitution.

People who live in India are known as Indians. They speak different languages, practice different religions and live according to the Indian Constitution.

India is the world's largest democracy in which people vote and decide who will rule. India is made up of 28 states of different sizes. It also has 7 smaller Union Territories.

Where is India?

India is situated in South Asia. The country lies south of China and Tibet. India has Pakistan on its west, and neighbours like Myanmar and Bangladesh on its east.

India lies completely in the northern hemisphere. The Tropic of Cancer passes about half-way through the country.

On three sides, India is surrounded by water, which makes that region a peninsula. The Bay of Bengal lies to the east of India. The Arabian Sea lies to its west.

The Indian Ocean lies in the south of India and separates India from Sri Lanka. The southern-most tip of India is known as Kanyakumari.

How did India get its name?

The name 'India' is based on a word, 'Sindhu'. The word 'Sindhu' comes from the ancient Indian language "Sanskrit" and is actually the name of a river. The Sindhu River used to flow in the north-western part beyond India, many centuries ago.

The Sindhu had another name, Indus. The region where the Sindhu River used to be is now in Pakistan. This is where the ancient Indus Valley Civilization was born.

The people who lived near the Sindhu or Indus River became known as Hindus. When people from outside began to visit India, they began to call it as 'India', based on the ancient name 'Sindhu'.

Why India is also called Bharat?

Bharat or Bharatvarsha is another name for India. The country got this name in ancient times. Books written centuries ago talk about a king called Bharat. He is said to be a sage as well as a great and powerful king. He was the son of Raja Dushyanta and his wife, Queen Shakuntala.

King Bharat ruled over large parts of the country. He became so famous that the land over which he ruled became well-known as the land of Bharat or 'Bharatvarsha'.

This name is in the ancient Indian language Sanskrit. In many regional languages like Bangla or Hindi, India is called 'Bharatvarsha'.

What is the capital of India?

New Delhi is the capital of India. New Delhi is in North India. When India became free in 1947, it was decided to keep New Delhi as the country's capital.

New Delhi is a big modern city. It has the Parliament of India and other important government buildings. The Delhi International Airport is called Indira Gandhi International Airport.

The older part of Delhi is called Old Delhi. Some famous attractions of Delhi are Red Fort, Qutb Minar and Humayun's Tomb.

Before the British came, most of India was ruled by the Mughal Empire. They too had Delhi as their capital.

How big is India?

India is so big that it is called a subcontinent, meaning that it just a little smaller than a continent. In fact, it is only a little less than half the size of Australia, the world's smallest continent.

Area wise, India is about 1,269,210 square miles. It is seventh in size among the countries of the world. India stretches across the lower part of south Asia.

Because India is so big, its climate, soil and geography changes from one place to another. The people living in its different parts live, speak, eat and dress differently.

What is the flag of India?

The flag of India is called the 'Tri-colour'. It has three horizontal bands in three different colours - saffron, green and white.

All the bands are equally wide. Topmost is the saffron or light orange shaded band. Below that is the white band. Below the white band is the green band. At the centre of the flag is a navy blue wheel with 24 spokes. This wheel is called the Ashoka Chakra and it stands for progress. It was named after Ashoka, a famous, peace-loving emperor of India.

This flag was designed by Pingali Venkayya and it was adopted in 1866.

Tell me about the geography of India?

India is a big country with a varied geography. The Himalayas form a wall in the north. The world's tallest peak, Mt Everest is a part of the Himalayas. The Thar Desert forms the western border of India.

The lower half of India forms a peninsula. India has a long coastline, on its east and west. Between the two coasts, much of the area is a "table land".

North of the table land is the Northern Plains with the River Ganges and other important rivers flowing through it!

Rice is the main crop of India. Other major crops are wheat, sugarcane, and cotton.

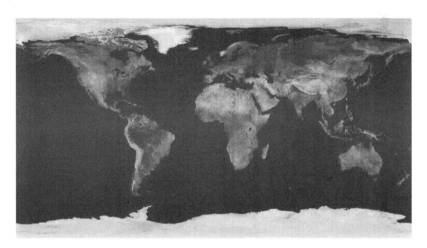

Which is the highest mountain in India?

The highest mountain peak in India is Mount Kanchendzonga (Kangchenjunga). It is a part of the Great Himalayas, the highest mountain range in the world.

The Great Himalayas have 14 of the world's highest mountain peaks. Mount Kanchendzonga is the third highest mountain peak in the world. It is 28,169 feet above sea level. It lies at the boundary of Nepal and India.

Mount Kanchendzonga is in the Indian state of Sikkim. The second highest mountain peak in India is Nanda Devi. This is also a Himalayan peak. It is 25,643 feet tall and lies in the Indian state of Uttarakhand.

Which is the biggest river in India?

The biggest river of India is the River Ganga or Ganges. The Ganga is about 2506 km long. This major river starts in the Gangotri Glacier in the Himalayas in North India. It travels across the northern plains and empties in the Bay of Bengal on the east of India.

Before emptying, it forms a delta in the marshy Sunderbans area. The regions around the Ganga are very fertile and a range of crops are grown in the area.

It is considered a sacred river in India, and many legends and poems have been written about it celebrating this river. Famous ancient pilgrimage spots along the Ganga River are Haridwar, Varanasi, Rishikesh and so on.

What type of money is used in India?

The currency of India is the Indian Rupee. Smaller than one Indian Rupee is one Paisa. 100 Paisa makes 1 Rupee.

The Indian government mints and makes coins and paper notes. The paisa (coins) are made of metal. They start at 50 paisa and go up to 10 Indian Rupees. An Indian Rupee note starts at 1 Rupee and goes up to 1000 Indian Rupees.

Anything that is sold or bought in India must be with Indian Rupees. Many Indian Rupee notes show important leaders of the country like Mahatma Gandhi and others.

The symbol of the Indian Rupee is given below.

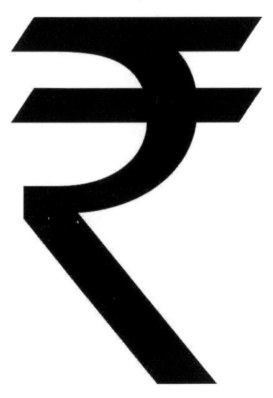

Who are India's neighbours?

Pakistan borders in the north-west of India. In the north-east there is China and the autonomous region of Tibet. The Federal Democratic Republic of Nepal and the Kingdom of Bhutan are also India's north-eastern neighbours.

India has two neighbours on its eastern side. One is Bangladesh. The other neighbour is Myanmar (Burma). The southern tip of India extends into the Indian Ocean.

Beyond the ocean, India has a tiny neighbour, the island country of Sri Lanka. Pakistan is bordered by the Indian states of Jammu Kashmir, Gujarat, Rajasthan and Punjab.

Bangladesh is bordered by West Bengal. Before they became independent countries, Bangladesh and Pakistan were a part of India.

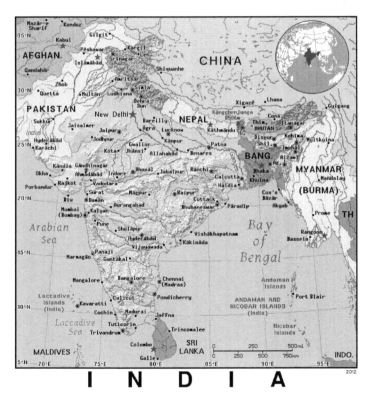

Why are Pakistan and Bangladesh separate from India now?

Pakistan and Bangladesh are separate from India due to things that happened in history. In the past, Indians who practiced different religions, used to live side by side like good neighbours. The British tried to disturb the ancient peace and harmony.

Not everyone liked the rule of the British. So the British tried to break the unity between the people to make them easier to rule. By the time the British left the country, Hindus and Muslims had begun to fight a lot.

The region of Punjab and Bengal had many Muslims. Parts of Punjab and Bengal was separated from India and made into a new country called Pakistan on 14th August 1947 just hours before India became free. Much later there was another war in 1971. After this war, Bangladesh was formed.

Jinnah, the founder of Pakistan

What language do Indians speak?

In different regions of India, people speak different languages. There are 22 formal languages in India. Many of the languages are very old and many ancient books have been written in these languages.

Hindi is commonly spoken in North India. Hindi is also the official language that India uses and this is the language that appears on many official documents.

In other regions, people may speak languages other than Hindi. Many Indians know English, Hindi and one other language, which is usually their mother tongue.

The names of some Indian languages are Tamil, Kannada, Punjabi, Malayalam, Bengali, Marathi, Gujarati and Telugu.

What is Sanskrit?

Sanskrit is an ancient Indian classical language. People used to sing, speak and write in this language centuries ago in India.

The name 'Sanskrit' means 'completed' or 'perfect'. Sanskrit is an important part of a famous group of languages called Indo-Aryan languages.

Today, Sanskrit is not spoken in India but it is the language of many famous ancient Indian books. It is called the mother of Indian languages as many Indian languages like Bengali and Hindi came from Sanskrit.

Followers of the Hindu religion have many prayers in Sanskrit. Universities in different parts of the world have classes in Sanskrit.

What is the population of India?

India has the second highest number of people living in it, among the countries of the world. The world's most populated country is China.

In India, different places have different population densities. For example, the desert has fewer people living in it per square mile than people living in the fertile plains.

Currently the total population of India is roughly 1.28 billion. The Indian state with the biggest population is Uttar Pradesh. The Indian state that has the lowest population is Sikkim.

Experts say that before 2030, India will leave China behind as the world's most populated country.

What are the seasons of India?

India has three seasons - summer, the rainy season and winter. Summer is mostly from April to June. It is dry and quite hot.

After this, the rainy season begins. The Indian rainy season is called the monsoons as the monsoon winds bring the rain to India. The wet season goes on from June to September. It rains almost every day. Bit by bit, the sky begins to clear up again.

The weather gets pleasant and less hot. Winter continues from November to January. Except in mountain areas of Himachal Pradesh, Arunachal Pradesh, Sikkim, Kashmir, Ladakh and Uttaranchal most of India does not get snowfall as the country is close to the Tropic of Cancer.

Is it really hot in India?

The Tropic of Cancer cuts through India and it has a sub-tropical climate. Many parts of India are quite hot and humid.

It is sunny also in most parts of India, especially South India. The hottest months are from April to June. This is the summer season in which most of India gets very hot and dry. In some places, the temperature rises as high as 45 degree Celsius and even more during the hot summer days.

People wear very light clothes, drink lots of fluids and stay out of the heat. In the winter, it gets a bit cold at night and people wear woolen clothes.

How old is Indian civilization?

India has an ancient civilization that is many centuries old. Historians and archaeologists have been studying how old the Indian civilization is.

They have been studying remains of old architecture, vessels and objects to understand the age of the Indian civilization. They say that civilization in India goes back to the earliest years when humans began to be civilized in 70,000 BC.

The oldest urban civilization was the Indus Valley Civilization. It grew up near the Indus River. It goes back to 3300 BC. It is a part of the Bronze Age of human civilization.

Varanasi one of the oldest Indian cities is more than 30 centuries old.

Why was India under British Rule?

India was famous in the West for many items like spices, silks, sugarcane etc. The British along with the French, the Portuguese and the Dutch were drawn by the wealth of India.

The British East Indian Company first came purely as traders in the 17th century. They got license to trade from the Mughal rulers who were then ruling the country.

Soon the company began to administer many parts of India, especially the ports and the places where they were trading. They fought with other colonial powers and won many wars.

In 1857 the Indians organized a big revolt against the company. The last Mughal emperor was driven away and India came directly under British rule.

When did India get independence?

The British ruled India for two centuries. When the British first took over Indian administration, they passed many laws and policies. Most of these laws and policies were against the Indians and in favour of the British rulers.

Gradually Indians began to rebel and organise many uprisings. The national movement began and many Indian leaders like Mahatma Gandhi, Lala Lajpat Rai, Lokmanya Tilak became important.

They fought to unite the country against British rule. People joined the fight in different parts of the country and made many sacrifices.

In 1942, Mahatma Gandhi, a great national leader, called the Quit India Movement. On 15th August 1947, the British left India and handed power back to the Indians.

CAPTURE OF THE KING OF DELHI BY CAPTAIN HODSON.

Who was Mahatma Gandhi?

Mahatma Gandhi was a great Indian national leader during the Indian freedom struggle against the British. He said that non-violence can bring lasting peace. His full name was Mohandas Karamchand Gandhi and he was born in Porbander, a place in Gujarat.

He practiced law first and went to South Africa. There he saw the poor condition of Indians and came back to join the freedom movement. He began many national non-violent movements, such as Dandi March, Non-Cooperation Movement, and Quit India Movement.

He dressed simple in a small loin-cloth like poor Indians. His famous quote is: 'You must be the change you want to see in the world'.

What do Indians like to eat?

India is known for its wide variety of foods in different parts of the country. The main foods in India are often made with rice or wheat.

Chapattis are a common flatbread of India. Many people also have fluffy plain rice. These foods are accompanied by side dishes.

Pulses of different kinds like red gram, black gram or yellow gram are common in India. They are cooked as 'daal', a slightly thick and watery dish.

Indians also love spicy curries, pickles and chutneys. In North India a popular dish is Rajma-Chawal. In South India idlis, vadas and dosa are popular dishes.

Why is Indian food spicy?

India has been known for ages for its rich spices. Cardamom, nutmeg, black pepper and cinnamon are some famous spices grown in India.

So famous became India for its spices that countries of the West fought to come to the country and gain control of the spice trade in the seventeenth century. With so many spices grown in the country, different places use different kinds of spices in their foods. Not all spices are hot. Many spices improve digestion, add flavour and make foods tasty.

Besides the spices, Indians also use different kinds of chilies in their dishes. This makes many dishes hot and spicy.

What is an "onion bhaji"?

An onion bhaji is a popular fried snack in India. A bhaji is generally a crisp deep-fried Indian snack made with a vegetable. It goes well as a starter before main meals. It is also great as a crispy munch.

Onions are chopped up and made into small balls. The small roughly made balls are dipped in a batter of flour and deep-fried. This makes the fritters crunchy and tasty.

Onion bhajis are often served with dips or chutneys. They also pair well with pickles. These onion bhajis is a popular snack during the monsoon months.

Many restaurants also serve onion bhajis with spicy Indian curries.

What is a chapatti?

A chapatti or 'roti' is a common Indian bread. It is made usually with wheat or other cereals like maize or jowar. It is flat, not too thick, and is round.

Wheat flour and water are kneaded together to make the chapatti flour. The bread is rolled out with a rolling pin. Then the bread is baked on the fire till it begins to get brown.

A finished chapatti is soft and slightly chewy. Chapattis are usually eaten with a side dish and sometimes pickles are kept on the side for flavour.

People in Northern India mostly have chapattis. Roti or chapatti is also common in Pakistan.

What is the national animal of India? Where is it found?

The national animal of India is the tiger. In the past, tigers used to be found a lot in the jungles of India. But, heavy hunting and poaching has hugely brought down the number of tigers.

Today, tigers are preserved in national sanctuaries and reserve forests in India. Some famous places to see tigers are Bandhavgarh Forest and Kanha Forest in Madhya Pradesh, Jim Corbett National Park in Uttaranchal, etc.

The most common tiger seen in India is the Royal Bengal Tiger. Its fur is golden with black vertical stripes. The mangrove forests of Bengal have several of these tigers.

Please tell me more about Indian wildlife?

India has many kinds of wild animals and birds. Elephants, tigers, deer, buffaloes, rhinoceros and gaurs (Indian bison) are some animals found in the wild.

In the water, there are alligators, porpoises (related to whales and dolphins) and different kinds of fish. India also has many kinds of snakes and insects.

The Cobra is a common Indian snake. Common birds in India are mynah, nightjar, crane, peacock and cuckoo.

Forests have been cleared in many parts of the country. Many animals are also trapped and killed for their fur, horns, skin etc. This has put several wildlife species in grave danger.

What games do Indian kids play?

Indian kids play many kinds of games. There is a popular street game called 'gilli-danda'. It is played with two pieces of wooden sticks – small and a bigger one. The bigger stick (danda) is used to hit the smaller one, the gilli.

These days, gully cricket on the street is also common. Kids and even adults often enjoy gully cricket on holidays when the street is less crowded. Kho-kho and kabaddi are a few other common sports in India.

These games are played in teams and there are matches sometimes. Other popular Indian sports are the carom-board and chess. Nowadays, many kids also play video games on their computers or mobiles like kids in other parts of the world.

What is cricket? Why do Indians like cricket so much?

Cricket is a popular Indian sport. Cricket was first begun in England by the British. It then spread to all the places in the world where the British had colonies.

Cricket is played with a bat and a ball. There are two teams with 11 players each. Each team has a wicket-keeper and a captain. Each team tries to score runs against each other on a pitch using complicated rules.

Cricket in India thus goes back to the time of the British rule. As people became interested in the sport, many famous Indian cricketers began to come up.

Indians began to like cricket even more as it became connected with national pride.

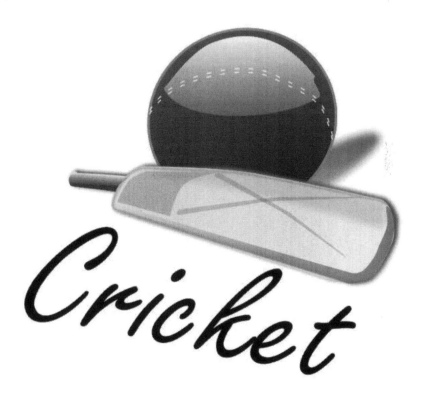

Do Indians play football?

Indians also enjoy football or soccer. It has been played for many years in the country. Some Indian sports academies also have football as one of the sports.

There is also a national football team. The All India Football Federation is in charge of administering the national football team. Different states have their own arrangements for football.

Unlike cricket which needs a smooth pitch, football can also be played in the rain, on muddy ground and uneven ground. This makes football a popular sport in India.

On days when famous teams are playing, galleries in Indian cities get very full and seats are sold out.

What is the religion of India?

India does not follow any one religion. People of many religions live side by side in India. This has been the way for centuries.

After India became independent from British rule in 1947, it was called a secular country. The Indian Constitution says that in a secular country, no religion is official and people are free to practice any religion peacefully.

The religion of the majority in India is Hinduism. It is an ancient religion and has been around for centuries. Many religious books of Hinduism were written in the ancient Indian language Sanskrit.

India has followers of many other religions too.

How many other religions are there in India?

In India, many religions grew and became important at different points in history. For many Indians, Hinduism is the religion they traditionally follow.

Besides, there are many minority religions and faiths in India. Jainism, Buddhism and Sikhism were also born in India. Christianity came to India with Christian missionaries in the early seventeenth century.

Islam also came to India many centuries ago. Many Islamic rulers came to conquer, but stayed back and made India their home.

The Parsi religion, Zoroastrianism and the Jewish religion are some other religions in India. India has many ancient temples, mosques, churches and Jewish synagogues.

What are the festivals of India?

Different parts of India have different festivals. Two big Indian festivals are Holi and Diwali. Holi is a spring festival where people put colours on each other.

Diwali or Deepavali comes a little before winter. It is the festival of lights. People light lamps, burst crackers and decorate their homes. Holi and Diwali are traditional festivals that go back centuries.

Many places in India also have harvest festivals at the end of winter. The harvest festival is traditionally just after the rice crop has been harvested in the villages and celebrates a good crop.

Onam, Pongal and Vaisakhi are famous harvest festivals in different parts of India.

What is the story of Ramayana?

Ramayana is an ancient Indian epic. The name 'Ramayana' means the stories of Rama, a brave Indian prince and hero. In most parts of India, Rama is also seen as a God. This story was first written by Valmiki.

The basic story is that Rama goes away to the jungle to keep his word to his stepmother queen Kaikeyi. He has his wife, Sita with him. Ravana, a powerful demon king who lives in Lanka across the ocean, captures Sita.

Rama fights to get Sita back. To help him in his task, there is the brave monkey warrior, Hanuman, with a monkey army, and many other interesting characters.

The Ramayana became so popular that its story spread beyond India to Indonesia and other countries in South East Asia.

What is the story of Mahabharata?

The Mahabharata is another great Indian epic. The name of this book means 'Great Bharat'. Another name for India is Bharat. This epic was written by a great sage called Vyasa.

The Mahabharata is a very long story that tells about the war between two dynasties, the Pandava princes and the Kaurava princes. Many interesting characters support the main people on both sides in this war.

Lord Krishna supports the Pandava princes and even becomes the charioteer for Arjuna, one of the important Pandava princes. Finally good wins over evil when the war ends, but the price on both sides is very heavy.

There are many interesting stories within the main story of the Mahabharata. One of the biggest stories, 'The Bhagwad Gita' is now treated as a separate book.

What is the Taj Mahal?

The Taj Mahal is a famous Indian landmark. It is also called one of the Eight Wonders of the World. The Taj Mahal is in the city of Agra in the state of Uttar Pradesh.

The Taj Mahal is built of white marble near the Yamuna River. It was built in the seventeenth century. The Mughal emperor Shah Jahan built it as a tomb in memory of his favourite wife, Mumtaz Mahal.

The Taj Mahal took decades to be built and completed. It has a big dome and four minarets around it on a large platform.

There are smooth and well-kept lawns around the monument. Every year, tens of thousands of tourists visit the Taj Mahal.

Is the cow worshipped in India?

For the followers of the Hindu religion, the cow is a sacred animal. The cow provides milk and nurtures lives.

Also it is associated with a famous Hindu god Krishna, who was said to be a cow herder. Many Hindus do not harm cows or eat their meat. Most restaurants in India do not have beef on the menu.

The bull is associated with Lord Shiva, another major Hindu god. Shiva is said to ride the bull. There are many temples of Lord Shiva in India. In these temples, the statues that represent Lord Shiva and the bull are worshipped by great numbers of people.

Why are there cows on the streets of India?

In India, there are many places where cows wander freely on the road. They are not harmed in any way. Many cows and bulls are seen especially in ancient religious cities like Varanasi or Haridwar.

The cow and other animals like goats, buffalos, elephants, and monkeys are also seen in some modern Indian cities. The cow is a sacred animal for Hindus.

Traditional Hindus do not eat beef, and let the cows graze freely. Many cows have owners. Since the cows graze freely, they often come onto the road and traffic may stall.

These days' modern cities are trying to provide protection for roaming cows without letting them come on the roads.

How do Indians travel?

Indians travel on different kinds of transport both public and private. To travel to different parts of India, there are railways and airplanes.

Buses are also common in India. Autos Rickshaws are three-wheeler vehicles seen on Indian roads. In some Indian cities, the subway also known as the metro is popular. In Kolkata, there are trams.

Boats and steamers are common ways to travel on India's many rivers. Some Indians also use their cars, scooters and bikes.

In Indian villages and small towns there are carts pulled by bullocks (the Indian ox). Horse-carts were also once common in India. Today, more modern kinds of transport have come into place.

What do Indians wear?

Indians wear different kinds of clothes depending on where they live.

The traditional Indian dresses for women are the saree and the salwar-kameez. The saree is a nine yard long cloth that is worn around the body. It is worn with a blouse. The salwar is a kind of loose pants. The kameez is a long tunic. The dupatta is a narrow long scarf worn often with the salwar-kameez.

Indian men traditionally wear a kurta or Punjabi on their upper body. The Kurta is a medium length tunic. The Punjabi is longer than the Kurta. They wear a lungi or a pyajama on their lower body.

Modern Indians wear both traditional and Western wear.

What is the national flower of India?

The national flower of India is the lotus. The lotus floats on water and has big broad leaves.

The flower has many overlapping petals and grows on a long narrow stem in the water. This flower is an important part of ancient Indian texts. It is mentioned in many Hindu and Buddhist religious books.

The lotus stands for many wonderful qualities. Some qualities associated with the lotus are beauty, peace, wealth and purity.

The lotus is also associated with many Hindu gods and goddesses. This flower is often used in worship rituals in India by Hindus. Vietnam too has the lotus as its national flower.

What is the national bird of India?

The peacock is the national bird of India. The peacock is mentioned in many old Indian books and is associated with Hindu gods. The peacock is common in many parts of India.

The peacock and the female bird, the peahen looks different from each other. The male bird, the peacock has a long slim neck and a very colourful tail made of hundreds of feathers. The peahen is duller in colour and smaller than the peacock.

When the rains come and dark clouds fill the sky, the peacock spreads its tail like a fan-shape and dances. Hunting the peacock for its meat is banned in India.

What is the national tree of India?

The banyan is a big tree and it is the national tree of India. The banyan is found in most places in India, especially the plains in the northern part of India.

This big tree has a wide trunk, grows over a large area that gives a lot of shade. In older times, people used to rest from the heat in the shade of this tree. The banyan tree has many creepers that hang down from it's widely spread branches. Often many villages have weekly fairs or markets in the shade of the banyan tree.

The Banyan tree lives very long. The banyan tree in the Botanical Gardens in the city of Kolkata is more than 250 years old. It is the widest tree in the world.

What is Bollywood?

Indians love watching films and there is a big place where films are made. This place is in Mumbai, a big Indian city, and is sometimes called Bollywood.

Unlike Hollywood, there is no big film city in Mumbai. There are studios in different parts of the city. Many kinds of films are made in these studios. All the films of Bollywood are made in Hindi, an important Indian language. Many films are made in Mumbai every year.

Some films of Bollywood are also shown in other countries. In different parts of India, people also make films in languages that are common in those parts.

South India also produces many films in various languages of the South Indian regions. The movie "Raja Harishchandra" (based on the Ramayana and Mahabharata), made in 1913 was the first full length Indian feature film.

What are the great Indian epics?

Epics are great tales written in poem form. They usually talk about the brave deeds of heroes. India has given the world two epics that are still popular in the country. One is the Ramayana and the other is the Mahabharata. The Ramayana is older than the Mahabharata.

In the beginning, the tales of these epics were recited. Much later they were made into books. Different parts of India have different ways of telling the tales of the Ramayana and Mahabharata.

These ancient books tell the stories of great kingdoms and empires and about the ways to lead a noble life. This makes them well-loved by Indians.

Did Indians in the past write books?

Many famous books have been written in ancient India. The Panchatantra is a book full of fables about animals.

A fable is a story with a moral lesson and in it; animals speak and do many interesting things. Hitopadesha is another famous book of ancient India. It gives advice on many different themes through short stories.

The Vedas are ancient religious books of India. The Vedas used to be sung in Indian society centuries ago. There are four Vedas – Atharva Veda, Yajur Veda, Sama Veda and Rig Veda.

The Jatakas have many stories about Buddha and his followers. Another series of Indian books is the Puranas. All these books were put together many centuries ago.

How big was India in the past?

Centuries ago, India was very big. Bangladesh and Pakistan were also part of India. Back then, they were not called Bangladesh or Pakistan.

The invaders that came to rule India, from the Mughals to the British, found the country very vast. India was made up of many tiny kingdoms and each kingdom had its own ruler.

Since there were no modern ways to travel, it used to take months to go from one part of the country to another. Traveling on business or to do pilgrimages took a lot of time.

Which are the Seven Wonders of India?

India has 7 Wonders, some of which are very famous in the world. The 'Seven Wonders' are situated in various parts of the country.

Meenakshi Temple in Tamil Nadu, Nalanda University site in Bihar, Khajuraho Temple in Madhya Pradesh, Konark Temple of the Sun in Odisha, Jaisalmer Fort in Rajasthan, Red Fort in Delhi and Taj Mahal in Agra are the Seven Wonders. They were all built at different times down the centuries. It gives an idea of how rich and diverse Indian culture and history really is.

People around the world come to see these Seven Wonders of India.

Which is the Pink City of India and why?

Jaipur is called the 'Pink City' of India. This is a famous city in Rajasthan. All the buildings in this city are either painted in shades of pink or are built using pinkish-hued stones.

The market-stalls, the houses in which people live, the old palace walls and everything around are done up in pink. From a distance, the city looks colorful in the many shades of pink. The pink city Jaipur is a tourist attraction and is a part of the Golden Triangle for visitors in India. The other 2 parts of the triangle are Delhi and Agra.

What is the national anthem of India?

The national anthem of India is 'Jana Gana Mana'. This anthem was written by the great poet Rabindranath Tagore.

When it was first written, it was meant to be a poem. Later in 1919, when India was still under British rule, he put it to music to celebrate the arrival of Queen Victoria and George V in India.

The original poem has 5 stanzas. When India became free, it had to choose its national anthem. This song was chosen to be the national anthem. Only the first stanza of the poem is sung as the National Anthem of India.

What is the national symbol of India?

India has several national symbols but the most famous one is the Ashoka Stambha (Ashoka Pillar). The design was chosen in 1950. The design shows four lions facing four different directions. The lions stand on an intricately carved base which has a lotus, a wheel and other meaningful symbols.

The design was found on an ancient pillar in Sarnath, a place in Varanasi. The pillar was set up by Emperor Ashoka, an Indian king who had messages of peace and noble living carved on pillars all over his kingdom.

The national symbol of the four lions stands for nobility, dignity, strength and courage. The Wheel of Law which is also a part of the design became the wheel in the center of the national flag.

What kind of songs and music are there in India?

India has a long and deep tradition of different kinds of songs and music. Classical Indian music was born many centuries ago.

North India has one kind of classical music. South India also has its own kind of classical music, which is also called Carnatic music.

Different kinds of folk songs are also there in the different regions of India. These songs are sung in languages that are common in the region. Many songs are sung in groups by the villagers.

Songs may celebrate sad or happy occasions, or major festivals or seasons. Simple musical instruments are often used with the songs.

What kinds of dances are there in India?

India is a land of ancient culture and there are many kinds of dances in the country. In various parts of India, different dance forms were born at different times. There are classical dance forms that go back many centuries.

The major traditional Indian dance forms are Kathak, Kathakali, Kuchipudi, Bharatnatyam, Manipuri and Odissi.

India also has varied kinds of folk dances that were mostly born in villages. Most folk dances happen when people are celebrating important festivals or on religious occasions. Many folk dances like the 'Bihu' in which large groups dance together celebrates a good harvest or other good news.

What kind of musical instruments are there in India?

India has centuries old tradition of music. Many musical instruments were born in India or became popular in the country. Many stringed instruments came out of India. Some few famous stringed instruments are the sitar, the tanpura, the sarod and the veena.

The tabla is another famous musical instrument. A tabla set consists of two small drums. The fingers and palms of the hands are used to sound rhythmic beats on these small drums. India also has a rich tradition of playing the bamboo flute.

During classical and folk dances or songs, musical instruments are used to make the performance livelier.

Why do Indians wear bright and colorful clothes?

Indians are fond of bright colors and pretty clothes. Since ancient times, Indians have been known to make many kinds of textiles to wear in different colors.

Traditional Indian clothes are woven in silk or cotton and use bright shades. The different colors are often supposed to have different symbolic meanings. Indians also love delicate threadwork in their clothes. In the desert region of Rajasthan, clothes are made pretty with pieces of glass and threadwork.

The hot sun makes the color of the Indian sky or surroundings very bright. Indians have always been inspired by the bright colors around them for their clothing.

Message from the author

Thank you for reading my book. I request you to share that you've read my book on your Facebook, Twitter and/or LinkedIn accounts to spread the word about this book so that more children will be able to take advantage of the information presented in this book.

I hope I've been helpful. If you need further advice or information, you can contact me from my website http://www.shalusharma.com or you can tweet me at https://twitter.com/bihar. You can always connect with me on Facebook. Don't hesitate to get in touch any time or ask a question. I will try my best to answer any questions that you might have. You can find my other books here http://www.amazon.com/author/shalusharma.